To PHILIP and

With love and best wishes
from the "POET-LAURIE-ATE

Laurence D. Cooper

LORD OF MY LIFE

Eden Press

LORD OF MY LIFE

Edited by
Rebecca Mee

First published in Great Britain in 1999 by Poetry
Today, an imprint of
Penhaligon Page Ltd, 12 Godric Square, Maxwell Road,
Peterborough. PE2 7JJ

© Copyright Contributors 1999

All rights reserved. No part of this publication may be
reproduced, stored in a retrieval system, or transmitted
in any form or by any means, without prior permission
from the author(s).

A Catalogue record for this book is available from the
British Library

ISBN 1 86226 527 5

Typesetting and layout, Penhaligon Page Ltd, England.
Printed and bound by Forward Press Ltd, England

Foreword

Lord Of My Life is a compilation of poetry, featuring some of our finest poets. The book gives an insight into the essence of modern living and deals with the reality of life today. We think we have created an anthology with a universal appeal.

There are many technical aspects to the writing of poetry and *Lord Of My Life* contains free verse and examples of more structured work from a wealth of talented poets.

Poetry is a coat of many colours. Today's poets write in a limitless array of styles: traditional rhyming poetry is as alive and kicking today as modern free-verse. Language ranges from easily accessible to intricate and elusive.

Poems have a lot to offer in our fast-paced 'instant' world. Reading poems gives us an opportunity to sit back and explore ourselves and the world around us.

Contents

Reasons

There must have been a reason why
All I did was sit and cry;
When all the skies above were grey
And the children went on in their own sweet way.

There must have been a reason why
I never looked at the clear blue sky,
I felt so alone with no one to love,
And I spent my time praying to Him above.

There must have been a reason why
I didn't even want to try.
But then I met You and You gave me Your hand
Now I'm walking on air, in a promised land.

There must have been a reason for
The happiness You brought with You through the door.
Now every month is the summer season,
'Cos You've shown me the way and taught me the
Reason.

E Mee

Where Is This God Of Love?

Why do you forsake me?
Where is this God of love?
When in times of deep despair,
No help seems from above.

Why do I have to struggle
And cope all on my own
With things that stand against me?
I feel so all alone.

'Isn't there one person
Who'll help me? Is my cry.
To lift this heavy burden
Too much for me' I sigh.

It would be rather nice to know
That someone cares today.
Not someone many miles from here
But just a prayer away.

So why not come before him,
And simply bow your knee,
Then give your fears to Jesus,
And let His spirit set you free.

Simon Martin

For Others Lord

Lord help me live from day to day,
In a self-forgetful way,
That even when I kneel to pray,
My prayers shall be for 'Others'.

Help me in the work I do,
To be sincere and true,
Knowing that all I do for you,
Must needs be done for 'Others'.

And when my work here is done,
And my new work in Heaven begins,
May I forget the crown, I've won,
While still thinking of 'Others'.

'Others', Lord, yes 'Others'!
Let this my motto be,
Help me to live for 'Others',
That I may live for thee.

Wm G Whalley

Growing Old

Things that seemed important lose their urgency and drive
As age descends upon us, such things are cast aside.
Our everyday necessities are all that we can bear
And the extras, once important, fade away on wings of prayer.

We see with age experience that life holds deeper things
To concentrate our energies and know the peace this brings.
To seek for higher knowledge and allow God's hand to guide,
Pursuing paths of righteousness instead of worldly pride.

Sorting our priorities and following after truth
Are the things that really matter, once distant in our youth.
But age reveals the secret that everyone should know:
Only in God's Kingdom are we safe when time to go!

Elizabeth Bruce

Human Frailty

Lord, if ever there was a time of need
it was there in the garden
when those first disciples, the chosen ones,
failed to keep watch with you.

Not one of the eleven remaining,
after Judas had betrayed You,
held their nerve and stayed by You
when soldiers came to arrest You.

Even Peter, the Rock,
the one in whom You had such hopes
showed how frightened he was by denying You
when pressed by those who held his Lord.

One by one, all
of those twelve hand-picked men,
friends of their Lord, showed their human frailty
in leaving Him to His fate.

Lord, we are all just
like the twelve because,
when things got tough, our resolve and courage
flee away into the darkness too.

Paul W Fleming

Untitled

After the bustle of the town
I came home and sat down
for a cup of tea, then thought
about the things that I had bought.
The tie I'd got for Uncle Jim
was it really right for him?
And Aunty Mary's After Eights
Is she still worried about her weight?
Or had she cast the diet aside
she isn't really all that wide.
I know Amy likes to read
but I wish I'd taken more heed
I'm not quite sure I got the one
she asked me for, but now it's done
the shops are closed, it's getting late
anything else will have to wait
what's done is done and so I say
let's relax and enjoy Christmas Day

J Powell

Immanuel

Sweet newborn babe, in quiet rest
Within thy mother's arms.
In calm tranquillity, serene.
Preserved 'midst earth's alarms.
Angelic hosts proclaim thee
'Immanuel' come down.
Wise men, from far, led by a star
Their homage to thee bring.

Across the centuries of time,
Of God's design a part.
Redemption's plan for fallen man
Restores his sinful heart.
Thou Christ art our fulfilment.
Redeemer, friend and king.
In thee we trust, and in our hearts
True adoration bring.

O Holy child, thou prince of peace
With carols, praise we sing,
The everlasting father's son -
With the spirit, three in one.
The earth awaits thy coming
This joyful Christmas tide.
May we, with deep humility
Dwell ever at thy side.

K Standley

You Are The One

You are the one who makes us happy
You are the one who makes us glad
You are the centre of our lives
You are the one true God.
When we awake in the morning
Our thoughts are ever of you
Through the day and evening too
At night when we close our eyes to sleep
Our last thoughts dear Jesus are always of you.

Margaret Fine

An Evening By Lake Galilee

By Galilee's blue peaceful lake,
    On ground where Jesus trod;
Was heard the voice of human praise
    Being lifted up to God;
As in the silent moments
    Beside a wave lapped shore,
In the presence of the Master,
    My heart began to soar . . .
As wafting on the evening breeze,
    Came a reading from His word;
And in that quiet setting
    The voice of prayer was heard.

In silent meditation
    As night began to fall,
And fishermen were gleaning
    Their usual evening haul:
I thought, 'How soon these moments
    Would soon a memory be,
But how wonderful and precious
    They would always be to me.'
So I thanked my Heavenly Father
    For that time of joy and love
And reflect, 'How much more perfect
    It will be in Heaven above.'

Ann Davies

Flowers

F resh blooms, scented, all hurt forgotten,
L ovingly wrapped in tissue and ribbon
O pening roses, carnations or tulips
W afting the air with pleasing aroma
E xpelling the low of sadness and sorrow,
R efreshing, renewing, romantic and real
S unshine celebration with certain appeal.

Eve Devenish-Meares

He Was Born That Day

A little boy was born that day, so many years ago.
Born to be our Saviour, the Bible tells me so.
The prophets had foretold of this, so many times before.
They had not said that it would be behind a stable door.

A manger He was placed in, lent by the cattle there
and all of God's creation came to witness and to share.
To share the richest blessing ever given to man by One.
He sent His only offspring. His firstborn, precious Son.

He came to earth to teach us, to learn to follow Thee,
to make that glorious sacrifice, He came to die for me.
So as we celebrate the birth of Jesus, God's own Son.
May we remember, reverently all the marvellous things He's done.

Yes he's our precious Saviour, He came to earth to win,
He came to give His life for us and take away our sin.
Every lesson He has taught us, every blessing He's supplied.
Remember that He came for you, and also for you, He died.

Trevor Rampley

11

Down Memory's Lane

My life began as a tiny cell,
In my mother's sanctuary;
Cosy, comfortable and safe,
A child of God's creation.

A precious jewel of rare beauty;
A bundle of humanity.
Full of life, pure and simple;
Destined for a glorious Eternity.

Arriving on a spring morning.
Surrounded by love and care.
Nature joined in the rejoicing,
As daffodils danced everywhere.

Life's changes as the years go by
As the seasons come and go.
Flowering and maturing slowly.
'Till life comes to its final goal.

M Dominique Aherne

Solitude

I sought her in the silently moving night.
     Not there,
People, thoughts and theories all pushing their way in.
I sought her in the peace and quiet of church.
     Not there,
People's needs and problems waiting to be solved.
I sought her in the highways and the byways.
     Not there,
Nature was upon me ever claiming praise.
Then right through those city gates I wandered -
     She was there,
Walking with my Lord whose love embracing all
Moved right through those crowded city streets and lanes.
     I walked with Him and talked with Him
And all their needs I lay at His feet while
The crowds like a mirage moved further away
     Solitude linking us both.

Elizabeth O'Mahony

God's Timetable

Man was made in God's image, yet how quickly he fell!
That he would yield to temptation, God knew very well, so
In the counsels of Heaven, before time began,
A scheme was devised to save fallen man.

Sin could not be passed over, God's justice decreed,
His holiness demanded a price to be paid,
No wealth would avail. For the debt to be paid,
Blood must be shed, a sacrifice made.

In Old Testament times, to deal with man's guilt,
The blood of an animal, pure and clean, must be spilt.
This was only of worth, as it pointed to One,
Who to die for the sin of the world, was to come.

So, in the fullness of time, God sent forth His son,
Made of a woman. The only One
Who could redeem us from sin, by His precious shed blood,
Free us from bondage, make us children of God.

He came as a babe, born in cattle stall,
He humbled Himself, although Lord of all.
Took upon Him our manhood, died in our place
That we might be saved by His infinite grace.

Yet He rose from the dead, nevermore to die,
Exalted by God, He ascended on high.
When God's time is ripe, He will come back again,
In power, and in glory, to take up His reign.

M Warren

The Feast Of Mary Magdalene

He cast out seven devils,
Seven deadly sins;
He saved me from the stoning,
From fear and dread within.

I bathed his feet with ointment,
Washed them with my tears,
Lovingly I wiped them,
With my loosened hair.

Some have called me crazy,
Yet it was given to me,
To witness resurrection,
His spirit rising free.

A Liles

The Call Of A Dove

Lightning flashed across the sky
Thunder rumbled loudly by,
Rain in torrents flooded the ground
And in the distance I heard a sound.

Quietly came the call of a dove
Hovering gently in the air above,
It flew quite near and brushed my cheek
It held a message in its beak.

The message said 'I am love and peace
I can cause all wars to cease,
If only man would turn away
From anger and hatred corrupting each day.'

As I looked again and knelt to pray
The sun had chased the storm away,
And through the clouds with radiant glow
I saw God's promise - a bright rainbow.

Jean Mackenzie

From Dumb Darkness To The Lovely Light

I cannot grasp or understand,
I cannot touch with either hand:
I cannot find the work or feeling
Within my mind, within my being.
I must seek out this dumb depression,
That shoulders me a sombre session -
Feeling cold and showering tears,
Bringing damp and fruitless fears.
It hovers round and tunnels through
The body spaces, old and new.
For goodness sake - just go away!
Leave me to live another day!

Dear God, I don't understand the way I feel -
I feel I have a rotten deal:
Depressing shadows day after day,
Tears and sadness in an awful way.
It doesn't seem fair to suffer like this -
When others share such fun and bliss.
Dear Lord, if You are really there -
Show me the sun and that You care.
Take away this terrible pain
That hurts me Lord, again and again.

But wait - oh Father, You heard my prayer -
My sadness is going! Yes - You do care!
I'm feeling better and happier too!
Don't feel so grim in what I do!

Oh Lord my God, my Healer and Friend,
I'm beginning to heal, I'm beginning to mend.
I can laugh again and see the flowers
That meant nothing in the depressing hours.
You are the answer, I know that now
And I know why and I know how!
I'll always put my trust in You
And Pray for help when I am blue.
Whenever I feel sad and grey,
That's when I'll kneel and Pray and Pray -
And You will help me every time . . .

Thank You Lord, for writing this rhyme!

Denise M Richens

Untitled

We have a God who understands; how good it is to know
That through each day and every hour
His love to us will flow.
His ever watchful eye is there, He never needs to sleep;
He is our Shepherd and our Guide, we are His flock of sheep.

He has a purpose for each one and if we seek to stray
He only lets us go thus far, and never all the way.
We'll never find a love like His
However long we search; and even though we're imperfect
We're used to build His church.

He's not working on a building but chooses foolish men
As bodies to be moulded to perfection once again.
And when his church is ready, with Lord Jesus at the head,
One glorious day unknown to us He'll come to earth, He said.

He will not be a Shepherd, caring for His sheep;
He'll come as King in power and glory, now to keep.
He'll claim His chosen people, whose robes are dazzling white;
They are the overcomers, from darkness into light.
The rapture and the wonder are a mystery today,
But all will be revealed, in His own time and way.

S F Wesley

Someone Special

God created, us, all special:
        He made each one unique;
He gave us talents, that we might
        Assist Him should He seek.
We are conducive to His will
        Each one of us fulfils
That special gift bestowed by Him,
        According to our skills:

He placed, on some, the art or flair
        Of caring for the sick,
The surgeon's skill, the poet's lore:
        The workman with his pick.
The author serves, God, with his book,
        The officer his beat:
The music maker and his score;
        The farmer with his wheat.

We all serve, Him, in different ways,
        We're 'special' ev'ry one:
The humble housewife, mother, cook,
        Others we sometimes shun.
There are growers, and those who drive:
        The guider, those who teach,
The shop assistant, refuse man;
        Or clerks, and those who preach.

But we're all, in God's sight, equal:
    Rich, humble, poor, or meek;
Each one of us most talented,
    God's gift for strong or weak.
As someone special, privileged,
    With Him we can but shine;
For through His power we are unique -
    God, be the glory, thine.

Frederick Hays

The World Jigsaw Puzzle

I saw you Lord today, at Diana Princess of Wales' funeral
You in so many different 'guises, in everybody.
Your broken heart being pieced together
      like one big jigsaw puzzle.
The messages, music all uplifting and consoling.
The healing presence of flowers, their scent and sight
      in your London gardens and palaces.
Your worldly garden jigsaw puzzle will be
      helped too by Mother Theresa's funeral
Your heaven on earth picture and healed
      heart nearing completion.
May I help complete your jigsaw puzzle
Thank you lord, with love from your
      handmaid

Joan Marian Jones

Do We Really Care?

Have you ever stopped to wonder
Do we really care?
About the folk we come in contact with
Those with whom our daily lives we share
Do we really care?
About the one who has a problem
And feels they cannot cope
With the things that each day brings
Without a ray of hope
Do we really care?
About the one who's lost a loved one
And finding life so hard to bare
Do we try to give a word of comfort
Do we lift them up in prayer
Do we really care?
About our neighbour
Who perhaps is all alone
And seldom has a caller
Or anyone to call their own
Do we really care?
About the one whose mental state
Is not quite what it ought to be
Do we try to understand that one,
However trying it must be
Do we really care?
About the one whose life
Is burdened down with sin
Do we ask the Lord to help us
To lead that soul to Him
Do we really find the time to listen
Or to give a word of cheer
Or are we far too busy

To lend a listening ear
Perhaps we feel we can't do much
To help another on life's way
But one thing is for certain
Each one of us can pray

A Shepherd

Flowers Of Spring

Snowdrop, why do you hang your head,
I think you are very brave,
To pop up through the pure white snow.
On this cold winter day,
Thank you, for cheering my day.

Primrose with your pale yellow face,
You ask no grand place to bloom,
Content in the hedgerow, to grow in the spring,
That children may pick you, and take to their homes.
And hand to their mums and grans.

Crocus, what a blaze of colour you make,
With your yellow, white, blue and mauve.
In beds in the park, or in small backyards,
You shine forth and say,
'Spring is well on the way.'

Bluebell, you have many bells to ring,
As you hold your head up tall.
In a woodland dell, you are a joy to behold,
And artists love to paint you on canvas,
You will look so grand, on someone's lounge wall.

Daffodil, with your bright yellow trumpet,
You have a special message to bring.
Your trumpet call rings through garden and park,
Saying 'At last'
        Spring has arrived.

Robert Warren

Forgotten Saviour

Though I'm not here, do you remember all
the loving things I said?
Do you realise the anguish and the tears of
pain I shed?
Though I'm not here, do you remember my
commandments for to keep?
Just one moment of your lifetime do you
think of me and weep?
In the silence of the night-time does a
question cross your mind?
Am I a person in your present, or a
memory from past time?
Do you want to know the answer? If you
ask, then you would find
that no longer do you know me, I have
simply slipped your mind.

Aileen White

Is There Anyone There?

Is there anyone there?
Does anyone care?
That I feel alone
Without a friend
Days stretch on and on
A road without end
Where is the meaning?
Why am I here?
Can anyone tell me?
Is there anyone there?

Yes, there's one who listens
To your every prayer
He wants to be your Father and your friend
Talk to him now
Tell him all your troubles
He'll be with you to the end
No burden is too heavy
No problem too small
For the Lord to carry
For the Saviour of us all

God is Father, Son and Spirit
He made you, saves you, keeps you still
If you'll let him be your friend
He will lead you in his will
Then you'll know there's someone there
Someone who hears, someone who cares
Someone who loves you as you are
Someone who guides you from afar
Yet you know his presence
Everyday and every hour
Know his love and mercy
And his mighty power

Georgina Wood

Searching For The Son

Some look through clouds and see blue sky above
Remembering the Father's unfailing love.
Others look through blue sky and see black clouds all around
And get caught up in their fear of being drowned.
While few look up and through and beyond
And recognise their Maker who is well in command:
The one in control
Who is Lord over all.

For although clouds surround and sometimes blue sky,
They focus not on the weather but, upon their Saviour on high
When the sky is deep blue, it seems easy to do
But when dark cloud sets in and it starts to get tough going:
They search and search harder for the strength to go on
And suddenly their revitalised by a fresh glimpse of the Son.

Janette Fearon

The Land Of Sunshine

There is a land of sunshine,
Beyond our cloudy skies,
Where resurrected people dwell,
And happiness never dies.

This lovely land of sunshine,
Is the jewel in the heavens above,
Where all those folk who enter there,
Dwell forever, in peace and love.

In our span of life on earth,
We must concentrate and strive,
To reach that land of sunshine,
Across the great divide.

Through the passage of our life,
Where Satan strolls each day,
Tempting us to break God's law,
And down a path of sin to stray.

Bad thoughts we must not tolerate,
Bad deeds we must not do,
We must obey the laws of God,
Laid down for me and you.

John H Hill

Mary's Poem

She was Mary, the mother of Jesus,
She stood 'neath the cross as He died.
I wonder if she thought back to His birth,
As she watched, as she knelt, as she cried?

Can you imagine the startling pictures
That must have come back to her mind?
Of the angel appearing before her,
His brilliance making her blind?

To be told she would bear a baby,
When, as yet, she knew no man.
And then to be told, *not an ordinary child,*
But her child would be God's Son!

To give birth to her child in a stable,
And from enemies having to flee.
With a child so young carried in her arms.
Their future must have been hard to see.

But now she stood under the cross.
Her heart breaking as she watched her Son in pain.
Blood running from beatings, from thorns, from nails.
She must have wanted to hold Him, to protect Him again.

We look at our children, when they are hurt or sad.
We hold them, we hug them, try to make them feel glad.
We wish we could take on ourselves all their sorrow,
And pray that the pain will be gone by tomorrow.

Mary, Christ's mother, would have loved as mothers do,
She would have wished she could take all His pain away.
I wonder, did she wish as she watched Him die,
She could have taken His place on the cross that day?

Constance Nicholls

And It Was And It Will Be

Let there be water
Let it be called pond
Let trunk and branch and leaf arise around it
Walling the sky's mirror against too much.

Let small plump birds paddle its silk surface
Their calls echoing ancient creation.
Let stiff winged things fly and dart about
Above stiff legged things that skim
A criss cross the water's top.
And let beneath flash silver through the murk.
Let it rise and ripple and vanish
In its other world.

Let sun shine and moon
Let clouds pass
Let day and night
Let wind and rain

And one morning,
When the grass is as wet as water
And sky, trees, soft breeze whisper
Glory, glory, glory.
Let a young man come there
From too much, carrying a rod.
Let him sit, savour,
Search the deep for silver.
And let, O Lord who said,
Let there be, it be
That he finds enough
Is filled and goes happy away.

Andre Fischer

St Boniface

Wynfrith the saint do we respect
 On this, the eve of Peter-tide:
A monk our Island did elect
 To spread Christ's teachings far and wide.

Born a Devonian, we believe
 In Saxon times, he's always held
Among the holiest men to breathe;
 This living faith and love to weld.

Now Bonchurch was a place he chose;
 That verdurous enclave in South Wight,
And, from this great and loved one rose
 The fragrance of a heavenly light.

He died at Dokkum, martyr he
 While quietly reading in his tent:
His soul translated to that lea
 Thence to our Albion it was lent.

He's better known as 'Boniface'
 Blest patron - said to 'move with power'
Apostle to the German race,
 A soul who's with us at this hour.

Andrew Newman Pellow

The Good Shepherd

The sun shone down on the countryside,
  And swept across the fresh green fields;
The sheep grazed slowly in the mountain air
  And revelled as they chewed their meals.

The clouds swept up across the sky
  And the rain came tumbling down:
The lightning flashed and the thunder roared.-
  'Twas the worst storm ever known.

The shepherd collected the sheep one by one
  And placed them all in the fold,
But when they were counted there were ninety-nine
  So one was out in the cold.

Down in the gully he went to look
  But not one was lying there;
So he looked round the rocks and under the trees
  But that place was also so bare.

He wouldn't give up 'til he found that lamb
  And wondered around full of woe.
But what was that? - A wee sound he heard
  And to find it he just had to go.

Yes! There was the sheep all tattered and torn
  He lifted it onto his knee;
And wrapped in a blanket to keep it warm
  He carried it over the lea.

Back to the fold where the others were resting
  He tended its wounds one by one.
Safe at last! It would rather be here
  Than out in the cold with no sun.

The good shepherd is waiting where-ever we go
　　And if we stray from the fold
He finds us and lifts us up into his arms
　　And to him we must keep a firm hold.

But it all rests with us if we want to be found
　　We mustn't stray from His 'road'
Nor wander where danger can cut us off
　　From the shepherd and His safe abode.

June V Mallender

That Still Small Voice

As Elijh I've tried to find you all through the day.
You were not in the wind of excitement, that blew across my
                                                              way.
Not in the earthquake of disaster, that tore my soul apart.
Nor in the fires of passion that have inflamed my heart.
But now as I kneel beside my bed, I wait to feel you near,
To hear in the quietness, that still small voice that takes away all
                                                              fear.
To lead me into tomorrow, whatever your will may be.
Yes - I find you in the quietness - when my mind is stayed on
                                                              Thee.

I Spencer

Conversing

A cross large and heavy you carried that day.
For us, you carried the cross all the way
Beaten and bruised with shouts of hooray
By people who hated the sound of your name
With courage you suffered the nails driven through
Both hands and your feet, if only they knew.
That on the high cross, you suffered and died
To save us from Satan, to give us new life
But on that great day when you rose from the tomb
You showed the world, that in you there was room
For love and compassion, for sinners to come
To ask for forgiveness for things that they had done.
The son of the father, begotten not made,
To show God's great glory, for all that he gave
We all carry that cross, but to help us you're there
Our troubles and problems to help us, you bare.
So remember that pain on that day you did take
I thank you sweet Jesus, and ask you to make
My faith ever stronger, my love in you pure
Until later on when, I talk with you more.

Patricia Helen Moore

Pour Down

Help me to trust you
Help me to believe in you
For I want to relieve
Into your palm
Anew psalm
That will take me
Through my trials and tribulations.

Poor down your love
On my human race
Poor down your grace
On my human race
So I shall win life's race.

All things known to you
All things made by you
All things which come true
For you alone see all
Being Lord over my soul
And spirit to.

Poor down your love
On my human race
Poor down your grace
On my human race
So I shall win life's race.

Holy Spirit help me to see
So I can open my soul to thee
Holy Spirit walk with me
So I shall always be
Concentrate Lord in thee

Poor down your love
On my human race
Poor down your grace
On my human race
So I shall win life's race.

Austin Satz

The Good Life

'Just give me the Good Life' I once used to cry,
I measured success by the things I could buy;
Material things were my food and my drink,
In a futile attempt to find life's missing link.

A sinner's existence was an everyday scene,
With scornful dismissal of Jesus, routine;
It took me some time and some heartache to see
This 'good life's' not all that it's cracked up to be.

I wasn't aware of the prayers being said,
I couldn't care less, save my ego was fed;
Then one day I went to the House of the Lord
And was shown by my brother the power of His Word.

I listened reluctantly, clutching my pride,
Not knowing the Spirit was moving inside;
The Jesus said 'I love you, no matter what's been,
Just take up your cross and I'll wipe the slate clean.'

I couldn't believe He was speaking to me,
But I swear to you now, it was clear as can be;
Without hesitation I committed my all
And gratefully answered the life-changing call.

Since that day my old life has sunk without trace,
In peaceful contentment I treasure God's grace;
And if there are times when I think of the past
I speak to Our Lord, and the doubts never last.

It won't always be easy, the cost may be high,
But Jesus' sacrifice saved you and I;
A wonderful legacy, lest we forget,
Let's not waste what was truly the greatest gift yet.

As my new faith now grows it's the end of my search,
I experience great joy when I enter His church;
With Jesus beside me, I've nothing to fear,
Brothers and sisters, the Good Life's right here!

T Doyle

Handing Over

The Lord has shown us kindness, he lives with us today
He's in our home and in our lives in every kind of way.
He's given us a conscience, to teach us right from wrong.
He lets us live in the world, but not for very long.
He teaches us to turn to Him, in sadness and in love.
Well He is our Father and He talks to us from above.
He likes us to read the bible, and pray to Him each day.
If we forget this sacred time, we will have to pay.
The devil, slips in very fast, and tempts us really hard.
But Jesus is our master, He knows our every card.
He knows the hairs upon our head, and knows our future too.
He will not let the devil harm what belongs to Him, it's true,
But Jesus our redeemer, calms the raging storm,
He didn't promise a bed of roses, or a gold paved path
He promised He would come and save us, and help us on the
                                                        path.
He promised He would break the bondage, and fill us with His
                                                        wine.
Jesus fill me with me with the holy spirit, the wine that sets me
                                                        free,
Make my body your Holy Temple,
I just want a life with Thee.

Heather Breadnam

The Birth

The angels sang of glory when the Prince of Peace was born,
A gift was given to the world on that first frosty Christmas morn.
A stable was palace enough for Him to lay His head,
And a manger where the beasts had been, He made His holy
bed.

The shepherds came to visit Him and Kings they brought their
wealth,
Herod sent his soldiers to bring his gift of death.
Love was sent that Christmas in the form of that blessed babe,
And when He stretched His arms in love He circled the whole
globe.

The world it gazed in wonder at the Christ Child's holy birth,
Peace and joy were present when the Saviour came to earth,
For who could tell that the Holy Child would be a sacrifice,
That He would stretch His arms in love and give us eternal life.

Ellen E Mills

Hymn Of Praise

Praise the Lord for springtime
all nature sings in praise
of rebirth to all creation
after winter's gloomy days.

The birds sing in the treetops
the lambs gamble in the fields
the grass grows richer and greener
as to the sun it yields.

Praise the Lord for the glory
spring beauty all around
hedgerows and trees are spurting green
bulbs shooting up from underground.

This is the time for planting
seeds to mature and grow
oh God plant seeds within us
of love that too will grow.

Margaret Badger

Christmas Again

Christmas, Oh no I can't stand all that again. Really all the preparations are such a pain.

I thought the birth of babies were supposed to bring such joy, oh look at him he is so sweet, did you really want a boy?

Aunt Flo sent me some socks last year, they were not it seemed quite new.

The elastic did not hold them up and my little toe peeped through. This baby that was born had no warm clothes to wear, His mum and dad did their best, but, it wasn't very fair.

Someone forgot to take the turkey out of its freezing place. So on Christmas morn a 16lb bird we had to face.

The stable where the babe was Laid was the only place to be. The hotels in Bethlehem town were all full up you see.

Grandma has often told of her Christmas' long ago, when in her Christmas stocking there would be a string doll and an orange in the toe.

There were some shepherds watching their sheep on a nearby hill. They were very surprised when with light the sky did fill.

The Christmas tree bulbs blow one by one, as they do every year. Where are the replacements? We've lost them again I fear.

The angels said 'Don't be afraid, we have such news for you. There's been a new king born, come and see it's really true.

Did you remember to tell uncle Bill that we would call round at eight? Because I think you'd better phone him and say we may be late.

They found the baby in a stable bleak with ox and ass standing there. The shepherds were so happy to see all that they could see, they bowed their heads and gave thanks in a reverent prayer.

I've brought a new pipe for uncle George, (he really should not smoke). When he lights up, it makes him cough and choke.

There was a very special star that shone out really bright. It led the way to Bethlehem for three kings by day and night.

When can we open our presents that are piled under the tree? Do we really have to wait for granddad to drink his third cup of tea?

The kings brought presents of gold, frankincense and myrrh. But baby Jesus was so tired He did not even stir.

Well, that's Christmas over for yet another year. Carols sung, money spent and far too much food, new year will soon be here.

I could forget that Christ Child now, but I can't cast Him from my mind. He was born for you and for me. He wants us His love to find.

I think as the new year begins, I must get some things straight. I must remember Jesus before it is too late.

He lived a life of love for us, though His life we did take. He hung and suffered on that cross for yours and for my sake.

There are hundreds of babies born each and everyday. But the baby born on Christmas morn came with us to stay.

Lynda M Summers

Friendship

Thank you for my friends Lord,
They've just popped in to say,
Are you alright?
And warm enough?
What will you want today?
How kind these people are Lord,
To show such love and care,
Could they be really angels?
And I've been unaware.

George Cameron

Friendly

I really don't want to be here,
I feel uncomfortable,
I feel people are looking at me
As though all the wrong things I've done
Are written all over my face.
And, even worse, people can hear my thoughts -
It's a really bad guilt trip.

They're so aloof, with their smart suits and such -
Not like me at all.
I don't suppose they have sins like mine to confess,
They all seem so self-assured,
            - Or is it smug?

I kneel down and don't know what to say,
So I hide my self-consciousness
By burying my face in my hands -
Like an ostrich really.

But my face is burning and scarlet,
My open back radiates wrong -
Why did I come in at all?
I think I'll bolt for it in the next hymn . . .

As the preacher rises quietly for the pulpit
I excuse myself crab-wise along the pew
Heading for the door.

The singing stops - and silence falls before I get there -
Frozen in mid-step, I hear a gentle but powerful voice begin in
                                                        prayer:
'O Lord, help me not to be afraid to speak to your people,
For we are all your children-
No matter who we are, how we look or where we come from . . .'

I find the end of a pew near the door and sit down again
The smart suit next to me turns and smiles -
Friendly.

'OK God,' I think, lamely,
'If the preacher can pray not to be afraid to speak,
I can pray not to be afraid to listen.'

Suddenly and softly,
A sense of peace and belonging engulfs me.
And I smile back at the smart suit beside me -
Friendly.

Philip Barker

Ponder, Wonder

Happy Christmas, joyful time
Sing to near and far
Of the Baby Jesus, shepherds and a star.
Ponder on the timeless news -
God loves you and me.
Wonder at the glory,
Christ's nativity.

Chorus:
Ponder, wonder, Jesus Redeemer,
Laid in stable bare,
Born to be our Saviour
All our life to share.

Shepherds watching on that night
Over lambs and sheep,
Heard the angels singing
As their watch did keep,
Ponder what they heard and saw,
They must go and see -
Wonder at the glory,
Christ's nativity.

Wise men guided by a star
Made their duteous way
To the Baby Jesus,
They must homage pay.
Ponder on the gifts they brought
All so reverently,
Wonder at the glory,
Christ's nativity.

Mighty God, the Prince of Peace
Full of truth and grace,
Radiancy of glory
Shining from His face.
Tell again - good news for all -
God loves you and me.
Wonder at the glory,
Christ's nativity.

Edgar Hucker

Kindness

I waited for the bus in the cold and rain
feet all wet, back stiff with pain.
Miserable, fed up, sorry I came.
Along comes the bus, almost too full
the old lady behind, gives my coat a good pull
'Let me get on,' with eyes full of tears
she whispers just loud enough for my ears.
She gets on and I wait once more in the rain
glad my loss had been her gain.
Many days later I learn from a friend
that my old lady was there at the end.
Puzzled I asked what did she mean by this
she explained that blessing has come from my miss.
By catching that bus the old lady arrived in time to be at her dying
husband's side.
When God gives a choice some kindness to show
never let selfishness make us say no.

Veronica Quainton

The Dream

I had a dream, a dream so fair, I was breathing purest air
It was to me a great surprise that I was seeing all the skies
They were so blue, the land so green, it was the rarest sight I'd
seen
I walked by hedges wet with dew, and everything seemed fresh
and new.
I smelt the earth, it tasted wine, I felt so free and lost in time
Of fumes there were no more, no litter on the floor
Of traffic there was none, no smoking chimneys blotting out the
sun.
There was no noise to drown the country song.
And I was happy just to stroll along.
There came a hill, so slowing down my pace
I walked so lightly in this lovely place
When o'er the hill, and to my great surprise,
Could I believe the sight before my eyes
Shining white below the hill, a small wee cottage quiet and still
The view beyond just took my breath away
And in this place I knew I had to stay
I tiptoed round and tried to hide
Was there anyone inside
What would happen if they knew
That I was looking at their view
It was to me a lovely fairytale
Until I saw the notice up 'for sale'
I quickly phoned the agent and was told
This property had long ago been sold
Then I awoke and crying
happy tears
I found that I'd been living here
for years.

Frances Crosby

54

All Seeing God

Do you know where God is looking
When he looks at you?
He is looking in your heart
Where nothing's hidden from His view

We who were far off from God
Have now been brought so near
By the death of Jesus Christ His son
Who holds us all so dear

Oh God you have been good to us
We adore and honour you
Father, Son and Holy Ghost
We fill our thoughts with you

Fill us with your Spirit, Lord
Do that work in us
That brings us nearer to your Word
Your Word in whom we trust

C H Bearpark

Moments

Moments are precious, Moments are
few, some have great Memories
some long overdue.

Do you have a Moment to spare
through the day? To speak to a
friend, or do a Kindness today?

A Moment is here, then gone in
a flash; I'm sorry can't stay
I must do a Dash.

Love in that Moment might make
someone's day; just care for
awhile and spare one today.

For tomorrow might come, and then
it is gone, then you're alone, you
just have to plod on.

Give thought for that Moment it's
a Gift that you've got; don't spoil
it today and tomorrow have not.

Kindness and love is a God given
sign, just try it today;
and the Moments are fine.

E Sharpley

Baby Things

How lovely are all 'baby things'
Small fledglings testing tiny wings,
Puppies with trusting soulful eyes,
Full of mischief, and yet so wise.
Frolicsome kittens at their play,
Enchanting, pretty, furry they.

Young, frisky lambs that herald spring.
Carefree, lively, gambolling.
Dependant human infants, frail,
Whose birth with wondrous joy we hail.
We thank you God, creator king,
For every precious 'baby thing.'

Evelyn M Deakin

Sunday

Where shall we go on a Sunday
    So many things to chose
Sport of all sorts, and shopping of course
    Also pubs, offering plenty of booze

What shall we do, on a Sunday
    After a busy week
Watch the TV with so much to see
    Perhaps news, that appear to the bleak

Where to go, what to do, on a Sunday
    Gardening it's said, can be fun
Planting and sowing, then see to the mowing
    Or lazing about in the sun.

What did we do, on a Sunday
    This sacred and Holy day
The years have brought change, some folks find it strange
    From the past, to the present way.

Shall we give a little of our time on a Sunday
    Go to church, for you won't go in vain
Perhaps kneel and pray, thank God for this day
    Find a peace, that we cannot explain.

M Lewis

Jesus' Tools

A joiner needs a workbench with many tools displayed
All the tools do different work for which each one was made
The chisel is for shaping, a plane for smoothing wood,
The hammer's made for taking knocks
The paint for making good.
Many tools do different jobs,
Whilst some do only one.
Yet handled by a craftsman make all the work well done.

The good Lord has a box of tools of varied shapes and size.
His tools are real people whose skills help earn their prize
So when you think I can't do that it's not for you to say.
God put the skills within us to use for Him each day.
If all men worked just as a team creating with their skill
With building bricks all made with love
And bonded with His will
We'd soon complete His kingdom as He meant it to be,
Using what He gave us thus making all men free.

Are you a chisel, plane or saw or a tool which shows much flair?
Are you the spirit in the level rendering all things fair?
Are you the drill, which probes so deep to plug and make things
firm?
Are you the wrench which grips so tight or the torch whose heat
will burn?
What tool we are upon His bench inside the Master's hand
He will use to full potential His kingdom to expand.

1 Cor 12 v 4-6

There are different kinds of gifts, but the same spirit,
there are different kinds of service but the same lord,
there are different kinds of working but the same God
works all of them in all men

Alan Lucas

Jesus Of The Manger

The shopping days to Christmas, how they fly!
The slowly-starving millions, how they die.
And yet if men could heed the Star of long ago,
Could feel the love that Jesus showed and help it grow,
The dreadful toll of needless suffering would cease
And man would evermore find comfort, aid and peace.

The story - is that all? - from mists of time,
Can bring this Jesus, child and man, sublime
In his great task of lifting man to love of God,
The Christmas Babe and 'man of sorrows', Jesse's rod,
To glorious, healing life which spreads love's saving power,
As souls of men, at last, awaken to the hour.

Yet Jesus of the manger, looking on with infant tears,
Moves on unheard, unheeded, as man misdirects his years.

I Smith

Be Sure Your Sins Will Find You Out!

One Tuesday my mother dressed up and went out
I couldn't imagine what she was about.
(She'd asked me to stay in and look after Claire;
I'd said that I would, but it didn't seem fair).
I wanted so much to find out her intent,
I followed behind her wherever she went.
She entered a garden which had a high wall,
I climbed up to watch her and hoped I'd not fall.
A stranger came out of the house and he stood
In front of my mother, his head in a hood.
I just didn't get it, but felt I must go
Directly back home, so that she'd never know
What I had been doing, but it wasn't to be;
On Monday my naughtiness caught up with me.
A wonderful photo arrived in the mail;
Mum opened it quickly and let out a wail,
For there she stood smiling, so smart and so tall
With me in the rear peeping over the wall!

Rona Pike

Who Do You Say I Am?

Who do you say I am?
Jesus - The Son of Man enquired,
The mocker dumbly looked and cried out,
'The question is irrelevant,
Why try to understand and go against the flow?'
So he laughed and walked away,
Therefore rejecting the key that could set him free.

Who do you say I am?
Again Lord Jesus cried out,
The fool just looked and screamed,
'A good man from history,
A person who lived on Earth, but now has no meaning to me,'
Sadly the fool lived up to his name and he too walked away,
Therefore rejecting the key to deep security.

Who do you say I am?
Jesus Christ did question,
The simple simply looked and said,
'A prophet who came from Heaven,
But what could this possibly mean to me a simple man?'
So simple just packed his things and he too walked away,
Therefore rejecting the key to joy eternally.

Who do you say I am?
Jesus again did ask,
'The Son of the Living God!' The wise cried out,
'The Saviour of Mankind!'
The wise will surely stay,
For they know Jesus personally,
Accepting the path of victory.

Questions ringing in our minds,
It's easy to walk away,
So who would you say you are?
A mocker, fool, simple or wise,
The time has come to open your eyes,
And see Lord Jesus Christ,
Asking you the same question,
'What about you - who do you say I am?'

Paula Aitken

Given Life

We only have one pair of hands
to hold the ones we love
we only have one pair of eyes
to gaze at heavens above
we only have one beating heart
to keep us all alive
we all have lips with which to speak
of ways of life to strive
who gave us all the lovely things
to hold to love or speak and sing
the unseen person up above
who binds us all within his love
whose hands encompass all the lands
from pastures green to desert sands
who does all this without a word
to us he is by name Our Lord.

Isobel Clanfield

Tranquillity
(Christchurch Harbour from Fisherman's Walk)

Peace, tranquillity,
Gentle lapping of sea in harbour,
Chimes; distant but clear
Transported across the water,
A reminder that time moves on,
High tide,
Boats, like sentinels,
All turned head to wind
Regarding the sunset,
The sky, changing its mood and colour
From shimmering white and pale gold,
Gradually deepening to orange, red,
Autumn fiery shades,
All reaching out from a ball of fire,
Filling the heavens with colour,
The Priory,
Stark - black,
Silhouetted against trees and sky,
A constant reminder to all that
God Exists Still,
All this panorama
Made By God,
Just lent to man as a reminder,
Just given to man to behold,
To contemplate; to borrow,
Just given as a reminder
Of what He can do,
Of what He will do,
Of what is to come,
Promises of what lies ahead,
Far beyond man's comprehension and understanding,
Eternity!
Another world,

More beautiful, more peaceful, more tranquil,
Full of happiness and contentment
And all eternal - everlasting -
Never to fade or change.

Joy M Kennedy

The Good Shepherd

Our Heavenly Father all around
You keep our feet on solid ground,
Our eyes are opened to the need
To follow the Good Shepherd's lead.

To pastures green He leads us there
Our souls restored with loving care.
He hears His sheep and guides us in
Our souls refreshed, unleashed of sin.

So heaven awaits the sheep who hear,
For those assured they know no fear.
The Lord is merciful with grace,
And those redeemed will see His face.

Jennifer Emsley

To A Poppy

That glorious flash that catches my eye
Growing mid fields of barley and rye
Standing erect with ear of wheat
And laying low at the threshers feet
Scattering seed for next years gems
To grow again amid the stems
Lowly and common yet full of fame
Witness to Flanders fields of shame
That man to man could so war
And blood of nations so out pour
Each petals a life laid down
Without fear or regret for the new world to come
Oh new generation of people born free
Remember the poppy-remember the poppy

O Crombie

James 4:7

A niggle, a doubt,
A thought slips out,
A twist, a turn,
A stew brews about,
Festering over again and again
Hold on tight before the storm breaks out,
Winds getting stronger,
Battling against the waves,
Slipping and sliding have my cares gone for the day
A muffled sound carried away with the tide
A hurricane coming all washed up inside,
A snatch, a grasp, a foothold at last,
To the rock my fears I relay and fast,
Thoughts that festered begin to pass,
A warmth, a lightness a love that lasts,
A gentle breeze with whispers to catch,
Dispersing with it a bad root to match,
A branch, a flower to fill its place,
Free to dance, rejoice and know his grace
To feel that warmth, that love from within,
To know Jesus' forgiveness has washed away my sin.

Suzanne Wassell

Untitled

Our walk of faith
is like the play of light
on an October's day.

Skies high
clear light
and birds calling
coldness in the air.

Then the sun goes in
our head aches,
we wonder where the sun has gone,
where vanished our ecstasy
of not long ago.

I recall a sister
of strong faith
enclosed nun . . .
remarkable in her
strange 'ordainness'
but such a stark
(such deep joy within) warning for Christ.

We are human, frail
and cannot long
bear that light
of ecstasy.

People await,
needing our company.

The TV question
said:
Name some non
- living things
that keep you company.
TV came first
in people's minds,
but just now it
deadened mine
and I nearly
forgot this
inspiration.

September is the harvest
of the year
October the stark month
of harsh brilliant light, then shade,
but oh what joy
in its maturity

Hazel Smith

Visions On The Way To Bethlehem

'Why do you weep, Mary, my love,
Why do you cry, my sweet?'
'I see a Man with thorn-crowned brow,
Pierced side and hands and feet.'

'Why do you laugh, Mary, my love,
Why do you smile, my wife?'
'I see the Lord laid in the tomb,
Leaping from death to life.'

'Now I shall weep, Mary, my love,
Now I shall laugh, my own,
To see your Child, mother and maid,
Make of the cross His throne.

Now will I pray, now will I praise,
Now will I shout and sing,
Because the Babe soon to be born
Is Christ, our God and King!'

Gillian Goodwin

Human Hands!

Designer made our human hands,
and variable in size.
Responding to the brains' commands,
and guided by our eyes,
those useful digits serve us well,
see daily duties done.
Expressing tenderness, they tell
of love and joy and fun!

Outstretched, they comfort and console,
all those who are distressed.
Nurture the sick or lonely soul,
see the young and helpless dressed.
And with the help of ink and pen,
to loved one's far away
our hands write letters now and then,
that vital news convey!

With love, sincerity, concern,
enquiring after them,
we read and mark and often learn,
so much from letters stem!
Yes, indispensable are hands,
their talents can surprise!
So many pairs in different lands,
called on to supervise!

Marcia Elizabeth Jenkin

Thank God For Easter

Can we believe it's really here
First Bank Holiday of the year?
Busy airports, extra planes
Traffic jams and crowded trains
Special offers bid us call
At B&Q and Do It All

Garden Centres - all deflowered
Chocolate Eggs - all devoured

Could He believe 'twas really fair
The grief and pain He had to bear?
Betrayed, humiliated, sorely tried
Deserted, taunted and denied
Then crucified on Calvary
To save the world for you and me

Purest Love - so abounding
Risen Lord - so astounding!

Eva Smith

Promises

Lord,
You never promised,
Life, would be fair,

You, never promised,
Life, without care,

Or, we would live,
On mountains high,

Linger too long,
You and I,

You, never promised,
To shield us from pain,

You only told us,
We would find gain,

Just hold us,
In your loving care,

When valleys dark,
Invade our lives,

Your peace will come,
The reason there,

Nothing separates us,
From your love.

Rita Hillier

Autumn

The leaves on the trees are turning to gold
Until gently and quietly they loosen their hold
And tumble to earth with barely a sound
To skitter and slither all over the ground.

The gardener then sighs and gets out his rake
To gather them up, more compost to make.
Walkers delight to hear the crisp rustle
As through the dry heaps they childishly shuffle.

The farmer surveys his crop in the field
And tries to imagine the extent of the yield.
The combine gets busy and little by little
The fields are reduced by bareness and stubble.

In church and in chapel people then sing
Extolling the harvest with gusto and zing.
The fruits of the earth are lovingly shown
With baskets of veggies so carefully grown.

Then conkers appear, each in its green shell
And eager young children excitedly yell.
They split them apart to get at their prize
Each boasting to other at the whopping great size.

Mornings are chilly and evenings quite cold.
The year draws on and is now getting old.
Mists are descending, the sun becomes fickle
Winter comes nearer, little by little.

But autumn is lovely, so let us enjoy it
With yellow and gold still here for a bit.
Glowing and brilliant for us to admire
Though not in this day with the harp and the lyre.

Smoke from a bonfire curls up in the garden
Fresh bulbs and more seeds our fancies do beckon.
So busily dig and carefully hoe
Ere winter shall come with frost and the snow.

J P Bowers

Hospital

I asked, and I received.
Another time, another place
Curtains were drawn,
in disgrace,
an Anglican proclaimed.

'The body of Christ'
'The body of Christ'
The Nun proclaimed
to each and every chosen one.
Drawn curtains round my bed
excluded me.

That day on Palms triumphant path
the King of Glory rode upon an ass.
An ass was I: too weak to say
'He died for me as well as you'
Body of Christ,
I shared in your rejection.

Another time, another place.
'I am an Anglican' I said.
She went to pass,
but 'Please' I said
'I need the life that's in that bread'
'Body of Christ' she smiled and said.
And all unknown as our hands met,
Christ's pain eased a little.

Janet White Spunner

Easter

The gift if child through pain is born,
Through pain of cross our sins are shorn,
Shalom, Shalom, the peace you gave,
To heart and mind of those you save,
Through love of us you suffered Lord,
You knew your pain gave loves strong cord,
To join forever, loves pain to Thee,
And draw us closer to eternity.

Ada Brookes Reid

God Of Love

Here is my heart given to you God of love
Many moments of perfect peace
Is enjoyed because of my Father above
No one else would forgive my sins
And cease to render me hopeless!

Lending a hand when needed
Is God's way of helping a sinner
Watching and waiting to be my loving friend.
I will not be weeded out by him and thrown away
But be a winner of his tender love.

God's gentle kindness day by day
Is intended for me in my muddlesome state
But only God in his loving way
Will listen, look and pat my pate,
Dear God, I love you so.

God's wonderful son Jesus Christ
Sent, all those years ago to be my Saviour
Allowed him to be crucified on the cross, priced
For my sake, his human body endured no favour
But rose from the dead to his wonderful glory, Amen.

Alma Montgomery Frank

The Soul Of A Moment

A celebration day pauses
As whispering hearts reach out
To link the nations born
So many years apart.
Fresh are the dreams of creating life
Earth and water stir in expectation.
A road unfolds with patterns laid
Designed within the eternal mind.
Nights descend but love transcends
To soar beyond the grasp of human reason.

Colin Bellett

The Circus

A Circus, that's what life is like,
And I the one who's in the Ring,
So many tricks to do.

At times I'm in the lion's cage
With only whip and chair
To keep the beasts at bay.
And then again I'm in the air
Tightrope walking (at my age!)
Struggling to keep away
That fear that leads to fall.

At times I feel I'm just a clown
And really letting people down
As I'm not what I seem.
For they think I'm full of gladness
When my heart is filled with badness
That only He can see.

Yet while I tremble, fear and quake
I know I only have to send
A prayer to Him who saves.

He's with me in that lion's cage
And stands before me there
To keep the beasts away.
And while I balance on that rope
He spreads a net to save.
My faith's in Him who died for me.
He died that we might live.

Margaret Sleeboom-Derbyshire

Thanks

for a partner

who cares for me when I am too ill to get out of bed
who cooks for me when I am tired after a day's work
who supports me when I need comfort after a disappointment
who allows me to be myself and does not judge me
who loves me despite knowing my weaknesses

I gratefully give thanks

for days

relaxing on holiday, lying on a long sandy beach away from the
pressures of work
battling through crowds while window shopping in town, then
enjoying a cup of coffee
spent reading a book when it is cold and snowing outside
enjoying golden sunsets and long cool evenings filled with
happiness and contentment
sharing with and caring for someone who needed more that I did

I willingly give thanks

for friends who come over for meals and sit and talk nonsense late
into the night
who I can call on when I need a lift to collect the car from the
garage
who telephone just to say they are thinking about me and want to
know how I am
who book for theatre and surprise me with tickets
who send a card . . . etc

I joyfully give thanks

for a God

who loves me more than anyone
who sent His Son to a sinful world to die so that I would not die
who raised Him to life again so that I may live
who understands my indecision and fears
who cares for me by providing everything I need

I humbly give thanks

Ian Macleod

Smiling Through

Sitting by my window or rather on my couch I recline,
After morning activity, cycling, visiting, gardening, is my line.
My years are many, my vision is clear, the smiles thru the
                              window I still hold most dear.
A tap on the pane and a smiling face,
Sometimes a dish held aloft, for me to taste.
Fruit from their gardens and vegetables too,
All these are given with their smiles shining through.
My first-born, with her dear husband, dwells over the way,
Their thoughtfulness and kindness are shown everyday.
The cycle is mended - my sheets washed, ironed and aired,
A tap and a smile to show how they cared.
From miles away, a smiling loved face (one of my kin)
Saying, Dearest Mother: How are you? May I come in?
Thankfulness and happiness in these lines show through
Making the bright threads glow in life's tapestry seem new.
You and I know as if written inside,
Peace comes from Our Father with whom we all should confide.
They that drink of Thy Fountain,
Never thirsty shall be
Neither shall they hunger
If they come unto Thee.

Margaret Gillings

I Did Not Know!

I did not 'know' this earth could be a paradise,
I did not 'know' until I looked into your eyes
I had not 'heard' the voice of spring,
I did not 'know' the joy it would bring,
I did not 'hear' the notes the love-birds sing,
'Til God gave you to me . . . I did not 'know'.

I did not 'know' the golden sun
          could shine the whole day through,
I did not 'know' that summer skies were ever so blue,
I did not 'know' that April showers
          brought pearly hues to sweet spring flowers,
I did not 'realise' loves powers,
'Til God gave you to me . . . I did not 'know'.

I did not 'know' the trees were dressed in such a vivid green.
I did not 'know' there was so much beauty to be seen.
I had not 'heard' the bumblebee go buzzing past,
I did not 'see' the greenness of the grass,
I did not 'know' that love would make me laugh,
'Til God gave you to me . . . I did not 'know'.

I did not 'know' the moon and stars shone brightly up above
I did not 'know' they were there until I fell in love,
I had not 'smelt' the sweet blossom on the these,
I did not 'feel' the gentle caressing of the breeze,
I did not 'know' that love could show me these,
'Til God gave you to me . . . I did not 'know'.

Linda Roberts

The Creator Of The World

I see his blood upon the blood red rose
I see his teardrops in the dew upon each petal.
I see his face in every flower, I see his
beauty in the sun's rising and its setting
I hear his voice in the babbling brook, and
the dawn chorus.
I see the touch of his hand in the beauty
of a clear starlit night - in a baby born
unspoiled into this world. How wonderful is
your world Lord God, you have crested every
beautiful thing.
Thank you Lord God especially for the lovely
red rose, reminding me of Jesus, and his
blood shed for me.

Elizabeth Hainey

Peace Concern

Peace is a trust: a trust from God.
Sincerely we must use it,
Use it for mankind's sake.
God of hope we pray for peace.
To our suffering and destitute neighbours,
May peace, joy and human rights
Not pass them by.

The ability to find rest in unrest,
The love of truth, excellence and goodness,
The free life of God's lovely world of nature,
Humility, purity and charity are all friends of peace.
To share all that with mankind
Would be peace concern in action.

An end to the avalanche of war clouds,
The eradication of racism.
Balance the difference between poverty and prosperity.
Find homes for the homeless,
A welcome and shelter for displaced persons,
Peace and joy worldwide,
As the new millennium is ushered in.
That would be peace concern.

Katie Kent

Meditation

Be still, my soul, think, and feel
  Within thyself is the boundless stream
Of life that ever flows as the fullness
  Of the tide, bringing God's presence
    Within thee to abide.

O, soul within thine earthly home, think,
  Meditate and pray, that God in his great
Love may teach thee day by day, that body,
  Soul and spirit are thine heritage of love.

The spirit as on ageless wings soars in
  Its flight of time and gathers beauty
That will bring serenity divine.

Thus the spirit knows no bonds of
  Prisonhouse nor chains but knows itself a
Treasure store of freedom through that
  Eternal bliss to come.

William Price

Cycle Of Life

Seasons come, seasons go marking passing years,
Seeds tiny, some almost invisible embedded in the cold black
earth
Lie dormant, lingering waiting for more favourable conditions.
With standing cold, hard frosts and blankets of snow.
Fingers of warmth waken their slumber.
Stirring the diminutive organisms into life.
Tentative shoots appear, deep roots develop,
Sucking in life giving nourishment from the unyielding earth.
Initially all new plants forms seem identical.
Cotyelyte leaves sprout, springing open delighting in fingers
of light.
Open to sunshine, kissed by rain.
Oblivious to gardeners worries of late frosts.
Cold snaps, in which life would cease.
Each plant stamps its own identity into the earth
Struggling for life, side by side neighbouring plants
Shoot upwards, flourishing, sprouting more leaves.
Stems strengthen, plants stand upright, straight and tall.
Growth halts, buds appear, the plants have peaked.
Fatter and fatter the buds swell, breaking forth in a rainbow of
colour.
Proud, upright, open to the sun, resplendent in their glory.
Multitudinous colours spangle the garden
Reds, yellows, oranges, pinks, purples whites, blues and candy
stripes.
Blue, such wonderful shades of blue.
Purply blue clematis, Lobelia in sky blues and midnight hues,
Petunias bluish, tinged with purple, delphiniums sapphire blue.
Stocks and ageratum, such various shades of one colour.
What wealth, what richness and maturity.
Drinking in beauty, becoming intoxicated by the sight
Scents emanate and mingle. I marvel at nature.

Blossom after blossom takes its place radiates and shines
Saturating bees with nectar, such a busy time, such abundance
for all.
Colours fade in the intense heat of the sun.
Receiving a new lease of life from the gentle falling rains.
Life cannot be sustained,
Flowers wither and die, petals drop.
Unnoticed seeds form, new life of each plant.
Life's mission accomplished, clutched tightly in pouches
Seeds ripen in the lingering rays of the summer sun.
The old plant dies relinquishing life's hold.
Knowing its life has been profitable.
Having accomplished the task entrusted to it
Living and dying so that the next generation might live.
Free, no regrets, it is able to lie as compost.
Food for its offspring when their turn for life arrives.
In the endless cycle of life, one grows, matures, gives birth and
dies.
The seed of life is then planted and the cycle begins again.

Teresa Booth

I Believe In Miracles

I believe in miracles,
Yes Lord, I do, and,
I know you do, too.
Please believe me when I say
I've got to get my prayer through to you,
In some kind of way.
Even though my flesh, is weak,
My spirit, wills me onto speak,
But lo', a thought, flashes through my mind
Why was your son,
Sentenced to die,
By an angry estranged crowd?
Congregations, praise your name
So lay down your guns and arms
You Irish and British sons,
'Tis all over for our young young ones
Please Lord, hear my prayer, and plea
Make peace in Northern Ireland, reality
I believe in miracles, yes Lord I do,
And; I know you do too

Ruth Byers

The Glory Of God

I see your glory way up in the sky,
Your glory shines on all that passes by.
It shows itself where e'er your Spirit dwells,
And echoes through the air like distant bells.

I see your glory in the shrubs and trees,
I see it in the honey of the bees,
And manifest in all creation holds,
In glory nature in your hands enfolds.

The sunshine on the waters of the sea,
The sparkling sunbeams dancing merrily,
The humblest of your creatures 'neath your gaze,
Reflects the glorious presence of your rays.

The rising of the sun on life restored,
Reflects the glory of the risen Lord,
The mountain tops in sunlight of the dawn,
Foretell the expectation of the morn.

The glory of the Lord shines all around,
In thought and visual image and in sound;
And earth reflects his glory in each one,
As moon reflects the brightness of the sun.

The glory of our God upon his throne,
Who gave commands to Moses scribed in stone;
Who dared not look upon the face of God,
Whilst there upon the holy ground he trod.

The sinner seeking help in time of trial,
The saint who seeks perfection all the while;
Reflecting both God's mercy and his aid,
And all this mighty world that he has made.

The sculptor fashions concepts with his art,
With thoughts of God's own glory in his heart;
Whilst author writing poems with his quill,
Expresses words of love enduring still.

In revelation granted to St John,
The glory of the Lord he looked upon.
Then wrote of all that he had seen and heard,
To make the final book of Holy Word.

In worship of the Father and the Son,
Who with the Holy Spirit, three in One;
The mighty universe with one accord,
Sings praises to the glory of the Lord.

Pius James Dapré

Ice-Rimmed Rose

Ice-rimmed rose, reflecting the sun
In crystal brightness your perfection shines
Preserving the taste of summer in the chill
Of winter come too soon - and soon to kill
All trace of colour and your curving beauty.

Ice-rimmed rose, your beauty is veiled
When caught in the drifting of my frozen breath
A wavering reminder that all is passing
Nothing in this life can be everlasting
Beauty must flee with the flight of the years.

Ice-rimmed rose, how short is your life
Yet to God is a day as a thousand of years
As he looks down upon you, a light in his eye
His pleasure is as though you will never die
But live on forever, perfect flower of creation.

Sue Robinson

Be Not Afraid

When thou walkest through the valley
of the shadow of death,
thou walkest not alone,
for Christ is e'er beside thee,
to guide thee safely home.
He will lead thee in his righteousness,
for his own name's sake;
he will comfort thee when in distress,
a bruised reed he shall not break.
He will lead thee 'side still waters,
there to take thy rest;
where other sons and daughters,
have been: and have been blessed.
He will strengthen thee in weakness;
soothe; in sorrow's hour;
deliver thee from sickness
by the holy spirit's power.
So come now; put thy trust in God,
let thy spirit sing;
for when thou feelest the valley's rod,
Christ will take away the sting.

Ray Varley

The Soldier Boy

Oh God! I beg You hear my cry,
Give me Your hand, and let me die.
If this is life, I long for death,
Dear God above, please take my breath.

You're all I've got, the rest can't care,
You are the One who hears my prayer.
Explosives and bombs fall all around,
And men lie dying on the ground.

I feel so lonely, helpless and scared,
I shouldn't be here, I wasn't prepared.
I wanted to fight for my Country and King,
I really thought 'twas an honourable thing.

The mud and the wet make me want to scream,
I sometimes think it's a terrible dream
And all at once, open-eyed I'll see
The sun shining softly, on my house by the tree.

But back to reality numb with cold,
At least I know I'll never grow old.
Escape from this Hell was never to be,
I'm glad I've got You Lord, please stay with me.

I feel so tired now and can't quite see,
A darkness is falling on all around me.
Now all has gone quiet and I feel that glow,
Lord hold my hand tightly, and never let go.

Anne J Bourner-Alderman

New Life In The Spirit
(Based on Matthew chapter 28 v. 16-20)

'Twas on a hill in Galilee
Disciples went, to Jesus see,
For He had risen from the dead -
He did appear, as He had said.

But, some of them were in doubt still,
They saw, and worshipped on the hill;
Jesus then said 'I have been given
Authority in earth and heaven.'

Jesus assured them of His power,
It was their most important hour;
They would with them His power take
And all nations His disciples make.

Eleven men of Galilee
Had a new mission, they would be
Teaching all men the Lord's commands,
They were to be His voice and hands.

He would be with them to the end,
They knew on this they could depend,
The Spirit would to them advise
Of believers who they should baptise.

We need no hill in Galilee,
For where we are He'll always be,
And, as His channels He'll us use,
If we give Him the right to choose.

For Jesus did the Father's will,
That's the task of the Spirit still;
The church, His body is today,
His Spirit still will show the way.

The church, it needs an open mind
And heart, if it would Jesus find;
With Faith that nothing can remove,
And love that will God's presence prove.

It needs a challenge here today -
If Christ, once more, will be the way
To bring the Kingdom, free from sin,
That God had planned, for man, within.

For every Christian has a task,
It is to give and not to ask,
To share together wine and bread,
With faith and life together wed.

Laurence D Cooper

Temple Hill Baptist Church

Builder, why do you break and break?
How can a temple rise from such a heap
From such a pile of broken people?
Can this be craftsmanship
Displaying all your wisdom
To the heavenly realms?
Will they do more than laugh
At the idea that these are living stones?
For all I see is failure
Everywhere I look is breakdown,
Mental, marriage, friendship
Always breakdown, builder, and I thought
You planned to build a Temple on the Hill.

'Stand back, for this is holy ground,
Downcast, but you are not consumed
For as you labour I will build my church
And one day you will see my craftsmanship,
My holy city radiant with the very stones
That seemed to crumble in your hands.
The ones for whom you prayed and wept
The ones that seemed beyond all hope
Are jewels adorning, trophies of my grace.
So follow me, struggling in dry ground.
Follow me, despised with the transgressors
And never forget I was broken
On the hill.'

J M Saunders

Wedding Greetings

May God grant you happiness
As you travel on life's way
Guiding you and leading you:
Protecting you each day.
May His love surround you
In everything you do;
That your care each for the other
May be His love shining through.

Dorothea Mary Clay

The Way Of Life

Every second passing by
Should be pleasing to the eye.

For every minute that you live
Be sure that you have love to give.

Hourly praise and thank the Lord
For giving us His precious Word.

Our days on earth are only lent
So take good care how they are spent.

Live your life, keep steadfast, fill
Your time and do His will.
Though the future you can't see
Our Lord has plans for you and me,
Eternal Joy He has in store
To live with Him for evermore.

Clarice Boxall

Unity

Divisions, races and classes,
Gossip and pride,
All prevent Christ's body uniting,
When united, in each other we could confide.

The youth are not a separate body,
The children are not excluded,
Age can not separate from the love of God,
In one united body, everyone is included.

Within our groups we've split,
Conflict has pulled us apart,
We all need each other,
To love, encourage and to share our heart.

United we'll stand,
Divided we will fall,
It breaks God's heart to see us alone,
When He's called us to love, one and all.

Yet still we ignore the lonely,
We wouldn't know what to say,
But God will give you the words to speak,
Just let Him lead you, all the way.

So encourage one another,
Let us all become one,
Don't be afraid to love each other,
United the battle is won!

Rachel Barnett (14)

The Moors Backpacker
(Seen walking in the Leck Valley with his dog)

Who would have thought I'd have backpacked now,
I'm seventy-five if a day.
I walk along heather and moor
And sometime the Pennine way.

My reasons you see are not what you think
I really don't have a home,
My faithful collie dog and me
All the seasons roam.

In winter we find a shepherd's cottage
To give us shelter 'ere
The snow and wind freeze our bones
In this barren lair.

Spring comes dancing o'er the hills
It makes a soothing sound
Gentler the wind and softer cloud
Than in the winter bound.

Summer at last on the hilltop shines,
Warms us as it glows,
Up we rise and on our way,
Where to . . . who knows?

Anon

The True Spirit

The country's in trouble,
The pound is too strong.
The poor and the homeless
Don't seem to belong.
There's fraud and deception
In all that you see.
Don't rush for the bottle,
Draw nearer to Me.

The car needs attention,
The 'phone bill is steep.
You're desperate after
A night without sleep.
From problems and worries
You'll never be free.
Don't rush for the bottle,
Draw nearer to me.

The roads are congested,
You daren't breathe the air,
The greenbelt is littered
With tips everywhere.
Society's crumbling,
The church is at sea.
Don't rush for the bottle,
Draw nearer to Me.

No time for the children,
No time for the wife.
No time for your neighbour,
It's nothing but strife.
Still more jobs keep filling
Your day constantly.
Don't rush for the bottle,
Draw nearer to Me.

For Mine is the freedom
And Mine is the peace,
And Mine is the Spirit
That brings true release.
So when life is not
What you'd like it to be,
Don't rush for the bottle,
Draw nearer to Me.

Josephine Gill

Sacrificed For Love

As you hung upon the cross, what went through your mind,
Did you wonder if there was love in human kind to find?
Was all the pain and heartache in your life worthwhile,
As they laughed and jeered and your body they did defile?

Pilot knew he was wrong but washed his guilt away,
Condemned you to death but to watch he could not stay.
Between thieves and rogues you took your place
But after three long days you left without trace.

As you now look down from your garden above,
Are you still able to exude the same amount of love
For mankind with his folly and his sinning ways?
For your fortitude and love I have nothing but praise.

Lyn Errington

Pentecost Précis

We have chained our God to yesteryear.
Nurtured the pastoral picture portraying His birth,
Savoured the stark and naked brutality surrounding His death.
It is, we claim, to justify the chaining.
A different country, and community and long, so long ago.
The world is changing fast: God cannot last,
How, in this age of space, can He keep pace?
Yet, can it be us who are the stumbling blocks?
We, who keep His chains secure?
Can it be us who do not, cannot move?
Imprisoned in cold fetters and have not love?
Creator Spirit, free flowing, free blowing,
Breathe on us now, thy sweet fresh breeze,
Blow from our eyes the dust which clouds our vision
Free our souls from their philistine meandering
Send us Your pulsating, Pentecostal power.
Unbind and free us from our chains
Make us move freely, changing with You.
In Your ever changing world.

Olive G Wimble